Night Palaces

Night Palaces

Poems

Rollie Erickson

Wordimage • ***Saint Paul***

Cover painting, *Dream Tree*, 2015, by Rollie Erickson
Back cover painting, *Day and Night,* 1986, by Rollie Erickson

Designed by Rollie Erickson

First Edition

ISBN 978-0-9994204-0-9

For Cass,

My life's muse

Author's Notes & Acknowledgments

This book is a collection of mostly surrealist inspired poems culled from a lifetime of writing poetry. It is divided into sections that suggest the passages of a day and also the passages of a life. The section "Dawn" begins with poetry I wrote when I was fifteen or so and spans about a decade to my late twenties. "Cirkus" uses circus imagery to convey a midday, midlife, set of experiences and reflects a more psychological complexity that develops with age. I love the French phrase, "Entre Chien et Loup" that describes the quality of twilight, and so I've placed a few things in that section that are more experimental, and are also neither here nor there (I didn't know where else to put them). The three sidewalk poems rejected by the city of Saint Paul was a call for poets to have their poems embedded in the sidewalk at selected sites (mine didn't make it). The calligram *Spider* has legs whose text is lifted from Blake's *Proverbs of Hell*. Also in this section is a group of portrait poems. A nod to Kevin Ayers for the use of the phrase "the liquid night," from his song "Decadence." This is the title of the last section and is meant to be the most quiet and introspective of the lot. After the poetry there are two essays. *Ruralurban* was inspired by reading Louis Aragon's *Peasant of Paris.* I tried to mimic his attitude although, in hindsight, I may not have been successful in achieving Aragon's subtlety. At any rate, it was an exercise in surrealist narrative and it is what it is. *The Inflated Tear* first appeared in Lycoming College's literary magazine *Brilliant Corners: A Journal of Jazz & Literature*, winter 2012, and had a full color image of my painting *The Inflated Tear (for Rahsaan)* on the cover. *Balancing Beam* and *The Snowflake Architecture of the Eye* first appeared in the *Asheville Poetry Review.*

Contents

Dawn

Cirkus

Entre Chien et Loup

The Liquid Night

Two Essays

Illustration:

Words do not lie.

—Paul Eluard

Beauty will be CONVULSIVE or will not be at all.

—Andre Breton

Poetry must be made by all and not by one.

— Comte de Lautréamont

Ah, this is the era where everybody creates…

—Patti Smith

Night Palaces

Dawn

Untitled I (1968)

When wandering long
upon a beach I stood
with
thoughts of all who ever lived
and how each face carried
a   name
   and
a   life

then when wondering
about myself and
life
and where it was that I should fit –
I watched a wave wash
one solitary pier
and then
move
on.

Untitled II (1969)

I like doing nothing

I let long hours
draw breaths inside of me

I let a small forest turn yellow
and drop all its leaves at the same time

I let clouds run free thinking
as large grackles cling to my wall

I let my hair grow

Untitled III (1970)

Well, it's like this you see,
that poetry I wrote about you
last Spring,
you can still keep it,
if you want it

Sometimes I wish I was
a fat 12-year-old kid named Chuck
with a blonde crew cut
topped by a dirty sailor's cap

he wears T-shirts
he rides his bicycle with
an ace of spades clothespin
clamped into the spokes to sound
like a motorbike but
actually it fits his
personality

Well, even if we ain't
making it no more,
even if we ain't riding on
Ferris wheels lit up
in the night anymore,
I still carry that lucky charm
with your name on it

Untitled IV (1971)

with the world smiling for what it was,

       and I,
           bringing back the flag

   from a dream,   I set out to write a poem or
song on tinfoil

      This, sad to say, was only my first
          encounter with a voluptuous umbrella.

        inspired by a fighting nun and two
           meat bearing trees, I had begun

my journey of two thousand miles (so I could
write my name on a piece of paper)

            when I was older they grew me
        a full head of hair, which was vegetation
made out of old radio parts

three idiot children tearing apart a scholar with their teeth

      it was then that I decided to become a blind man
          watching TV

Untitled V (self-portrait at 25)

If flowers are read
why not prop them with bookends
stacked tattered leaves from a
child's yellowed primer
vacant in the eyes of a Midwestern
preacher searching for Truth
in the folds of a nun.
This poem is for you who was
seventeen
and thought that the world could be
simple and fun.
Your mother is harmless now
and your father has doubled.
Truth has been strange but
your tongue's still in cheek.
Clouds, stars, and dogs
still tattoo your ideas and love
comes as often as always.
Dreaming is God's gift
if we can call it that
(or Him "It")
and money
burns holes
in your pocket.

Valentine

i had an affair with a tree once
whose shoulders stretched broad
and high in blue wind; no branches
bent low enough to break or yield
fealty to the conquering grip
of a child's hands – a trunk
insurmountable
other kids thought i was nuts to claim it
(as my own) but
years later
as they mounted their careers
and the limbs of their
husbands and wives
all the trees in that park were cut
down first by elm-worm
next by saw
none left except my one (true story)
so why is this a valentine?
i don't know
but delight and strength
marks the fabric of our weave
standing like my tree against
all odds as if to say
i love you
for all the world to see

Having You

Just having you there to say
yes the earth is red is
more than enough more
than a theory for you
to say yes to me that the
earth is green is more
than enough for me more
than a mere speculation
to have you here and say
yes to me
that the world is indeed robed
in a lavender light that
no, you are not guessing
it's a fact and you are here
saying yes to me
that the whole goddamn planet
is more than
life black
or more than
death white
that it's yes
on a tightrope
pirouetting
into night.

Pelvis

All snakes were once roots
that found their freedom through a thirst
for fire.
The antique venom dispels a menace
of ladders for the woman whose face
opens the iris trembling
like a street lamp against a moth.
The man, woven from fronds of hemlock,
offers the hands cupped one
into the other,
holding the invisible and sacred
hollow of your throat
    (what is it called?)
where a watermelon seed
sits perfectly
& the camphor lips of dawn
drink the ground.

Subway

wartime in the heart
and a stranger in your eyes
whoever said that
goodbyes meant the same as
"till we meet again?"
(to affirm an afterlife)
from my corner of the world
I have watched you slip
into as many lies as reality
can afford for comfort
turning love into something dumb
and breathless
and an invitation
to a riot while
real life
abides in the unexpected
and will embrace you
like an eviction
—we carry our flesh like a river
yielding to a bedrock of bones
we walk from day to brilliant day
through tunnels carved
in the night by our dreaming—
but as for me,
tell my friends I've gone riding
down deep into Kore's Underworld
where a child cries
on the D line in sobs
of pure Coltrane

Cirkus

Big Top

In the blackness of its pinwheel heart
the white dawn unmasks
a cotillion of naked angels
where the king pole of the big top draws
the attention of the crowd
to the trapeze of a fire snake that points
at true magnetic north, a circle of cold fire;
the Ferris wheel for those who sleep
and dream themselves to be the fleas that
bite the apes who pulverize this country.

Give me the cold blue of diamond dust
the steel pierce of the midnight shriek
a forest made entirely of crystal
where the leaves are thin green lips
and our hands are quick to bite...

here

where the squirrel is the silverfish of trees
and the insects extremely well dressed.
Larkspur cadavers drink invisible words
from rusted cups of jade and cinnabar
while an egret enchanted with quicksilver
                    lays vowels into the
                    symbols of a closing
                    century.

The ringmaster drifts into a pool of light
and with an outstretched hand bellows
like a preacher, a holy carney barker:

Come one, come all!
Those who are not of this earth,
you who are the witnesses of a true and
awful pleasure! Our language pukes of
history. Watch it as it rolls into a ball
and the seals toss it into the depths of your
spines, watch as the acrobats
wearing only the eyeless masks of night
sprout roots from these vanquished
branches revealing those invisible birds;
        and the tail prehensile
that sinks
        and takes root
                gnashing its teeth!

Balancing Beam

A miniature black coach pulled by a team
of tiny black horses, glinting the names of the dead
from their tiny white teeth and the exquisite
little shadows that drive the wagon laugh,
snapping the whip before your eyes daring
you to recognize their faces daring
you to take a closer look
on the darkened road of your choice
from the silence of trees made of one leaf
you stand on one foot balanced
clutching a mirror full of goldfish and a mask
whose eyes are lips whispering the intimacies
of your skeleton swept from the night of the forest
floor giving wing to the foot of a flight of stairs
where the hat is a club crowning the head
and the solipsism of a waterfall creates
a specter of innocence.
Those are smoke-filled rooms that bruise the sky
the sun going down to its watery grave
the eyes that are poppies swaying in the breeze
in the hair of a fine toothed snow
at the bottom of a lake
a glissade before the toe
where we read in the
History of Doves that
the birds fish for clues
obeying the
perch

Evol

evolution is a slow think –
to simply be, was that not enough?
that which is seen becoming from
that which is unseen
as an airplane feasts
in an artificial garden where
Blood Root
hemorrhages a water star for the solar
sea horse and the crickets
devour silence like a flame threatened
by the black dance
of moths
the pale skinned women of the Arctic
stroke their beards
enflamed by the slightest gesture of the sea...
they sing a patriotic song to a young
and reckless glass of milk while
the forest opens
like a giant lotus becoming
the first vowel
ever uttered...
                  whose ashes are these
the cracks of the earth betray?
a secret lightning of hidden laughter
opens to the ancestry
of chance
and sacrifice
for god or no god
the marigolds will dance

on the dust of your days
congealed
with a mixture of
future blood and
ancient honey

Snowlight

Rimbaud's skies are in descent,
chandelier's opaque and cantilevered
from the azure eyes that focus
like a pilot light gripping the air
with its teeth
here a taxonomy of birds freeze into crystal
surpassing even themselves in a
life or death waltz

Water is the color of air
each movement redolent of memory
hands cupped to the face revealing the mask
of vast landscapes just beneath its surface
where Winter is in excess of Spring's
suicides and thought is an assumption
inside a small cradle of bones

Stones are the locked secret memory of place
a white stone slipped naked beneath the river
of your tongue where swans tuck
and roll the black water from their backs
like a pair of hands dipped into a china basin
hands placed in supplication
enfolding the sacred motion of flight
through the open silence of a window

The vertebrae of a cottage lingers
on the brow of an elephant
in a corridor where the wings of a mayfly

shimmer open and shut
open and shut tight
like a chestnut
inside a small cradle of bones
where the history of the tree
is given from the worm's eye view
at very high speed
and in reverse
turning its blind blood into the wind
opened from a weather vein

Snowlight casts itself without shadows
a gloom of light insinuating safe passage
for the circus woman with antlers devouring
the innocence of cannibal trees
and the matrix wolf of black mirrors hopping
like a frightened child with a dead bird
in its mouth
inside a small cradle of bones

Snowlight inchoate with the white mistress
(I slip a knife into the dictionary
hoping to discover her name)
the fruit opens with a bang as orphans
display an ossified carriage meant to cauterize
the movement of rain
frozen at any given moment into
prisms of tears that tear at the sky
like a patch of milk
in this charred flesh
this fish bone forest

The honesty of a ventriloquist
paints the portrait of an estuary
as snowlight piths the visage
of an ordinary day
with a single-handed stroke of the clock that grasps
the darkness lit by a calla lily
the paper plate leaves of the calathea
rotate invisibly on the somnambulant feet
of sea urchins
whose circumference is a white ovulate
that gets digested in seconds
and quite without reason
inside a small cradle of bones

The Ringmaster's Hat

The little fire engine inside the snail's shell

is a carousel for the otter's teeth

sunk deep into the eye of a beguiled

and bearded infant.

Such is the hinge of the world as it groans

from an enormous and perpetual weight

of black wind, from the weight

of an elephant whose head is the sun,

from the weight of a street address penciled

on her lips that darkle in an artery of shadow

from the weight of my shoes in p.s.i.

and at sea-level

where the blossoming squid run in rivulets of green

diamonds in the ruby eyed bruise of evening—

Let the empty coat hanger sing:

How does one disassociate fear from pain? The will to flee
is carried over into the dream at the slightest hint of danger
since the dream draws from the day. But why does one
suffer from pain not felt, only expected? The poet/assassin is
offered a cup of wind that blows forth the seeds of milkweed.
Someone has left a hat. A loaf of bread with a hole cut into

*the side, placed perfectly on the head of the poet/assassin
who is threatened by a cadre of men lurking in the hall (just
like in the painting). They move in closer. In the mayhem, a
knife unfolds.*

They told me I could not say it in this way

that what you expect

is what you hallucinate and that

every brick is mortared with the thoughts

of those who built these walls.

They, whose image fades beneath

the ruggedness of this medusan sun,

while the agony of the grass dispels the riot

of its leaves in a fossilized forest known

for its standard of glass breasts.

The birds of a nearby town build nests

made of echoes and lay eggs

that resemble wizened planets,

or the pallid eyes of a frozen insect.

The narcotic flight of my gloved hand

circumscribes the dawn,

where the eyes of the Ibis,

observe the entrails on a divination tray

and where the lantern-song of the moth

skips rope with a tightrope walker,

whose rectrix is aligned in a room made of wind –

Let the dung beetle roll the earth:

In the dissolvable distance, one may disassociate the memory of an item from the thing itself. The wall is now penetrable, breathing through its pores like a sponge, and the door no longer opens. The frightened street presses questions into a box while the sky, which was never blue, cheats at cards. Into this ring I toss my hat. My drink of choice is made from the fire in an eagle's eye, from a femur in the limbed darkness of the air. And the light? The light makes a web of the bare branches encircled with globules of water—a cosmos of water planets and stars that decipher the spectrum secrets of the sun.

In the forest of my heart,

in the sanguine venation of

it's violent leaves,

the idol carves itself

with a laugh and a craving

that is quite meticulous,

ruthless,

and frighteningly

lifelike

Whites of Their Eyes

Given the devout play of the anesthetist's collection
    of small stones
           and the white call of the crow

Given the tentacled maple that hoists
    its leaves like a woman drawing
          nylons to her thighs

Given the fact that I cannot breathe
    or dare not when the ermine is young
        and feeding like a cannibal with
           a fine tincture of granite

Given the flowering gut of a rabbit
    that rises like an island when an ibis
        pulls up a corner of the sea
          exposing the legs of a pope

Given the fact that before there were cathedrals
    there were caves and before caves
        there was Night and within
          the night there arose the
        stained glass stars
        of objective chance
Then –
    the air becomes opened and clear
        and the path finds me –
        before I am on it

Saltimbanques

Saturated with the silver of vowels
we who have caressed a hyacinth of stars
speak remotely with a tongue of mercury
carried in the womb of a bird

Somewhere in the augury of shadows
a man and woman made entirely of fir
light the lamps that encircle the city
and open the temples for a worshipped earth

Knowing that water is the absence of habit
the horned ones play at the mouth of experience
bells garnish the wind while bones dance
a simulacrum of mathematical reality

They are the ones with alphabets for eyes
they are the animals that walk on water
the hummingbird heart that melts the glacier
they tumble into perfect geometries

The fire breathed from the mouth is worth more
than the cutlery of drunken geese
the impossible tome of the sky is worth
more than the annihilation of its color

Take a knife, a bell, a midnight star
and pour them from a bottle green with flame
the wine is like a window to the sea
and freedom a door banging in the wind

Orbo, the Dog-faced Boy

I was dancing with the dogs at century's turn
where infant lightning betrays the ragged
cloak of human kindness
forests of calculations entomb the houses at sunrise
and the mermaids unstring their harps
for a Black Sea wedding

the window is open
and I'm almost naked

my lips that are green with one eye violet
my voice orange from indigo talking
tongue made of feldspar
hair of blue marble fire
I am no longer here (and
the dotted "i" is the one that weeps)
the iron gate of my face has lifted
but the dog is no longer there

the window is open
and I'm almost naked

the innocence of the little dictators smelling
gently of gunpowder, lost teeth
and the romance of another world war
roars like a flint strike to the gas line
of my heart
into the lions of oblivion
the International Standard of Slums
forks over the unclaimed cadavers
who smile at the loss
of their own shadow

the window is open

the window that jives and struts
like a pirate on steroids
like a flesh form eating dazzle
neon pink obliteration of
permanent snow-blind escape
I mean to say my dilated pupil
where I'm forced to drop
                              one shoe
                    one hat
              one coat
         one set of keys

Clown Time

I have this friend who
can't speak for himself
he can't speak
but he would like to tell you all
to go take a flying fuck
(squeezing the bulb of his duck)
he can't talk well enough
he can't talk
well enough to say it himself
but half the time wishes for
you-know-what
(A Little Death)
or a tiny mirror for his shoes
to slip under your skirt
(and that would make his flower squirt)
my friend I guess you could say
has a problem
or a grievance
I guess you could
but really he would
need only a small-wee-bit
of your time
if you could spare it
if you can spare the time
he would like to say…
     and wiping his white face away

in the light from a single bulb
above his head
(wavering like an idea)
"go to hell all of you
 go fuck yourselves"
if he could talk
(and paddling his Chaplin
feet) telling you
that if
he could live
on the ceiling of your room
then his floor would be
quite clean
thank you
there's the door
(you are excused)

Myth

The ceiling fans were some slow
wings of dragonflies
fat and iridescently unhurried
the buzz and hollow
of its wings
a universe unfolding
stretching black and
kinematic
where the dreamer drifts…

we see the hunter
the sporting Hero who
would track the wounded
beast in the sanguine snow
– down by the unlucky
farmhouse go –
O save the women and children!
and save the cattle too!
But with his vestige too wet
and heavy with the kill
he's unable to even recognize
The Beast
who is not of our time
who thinks outside
of ourselves
with its shimmering voice
it ties our stomachs in knots
shhh…
if it turns and catches your gaze
then there's nothing
on earth
could it stop

Spell

A simple wish,
a desire to be wicked—
and so a form became a person
and engaged me with their neck
to my claw
it was so easy
I drowned them and wore their skeleton
for a necktie
but one must work for The Descent
and an amiable door witnessed with such
ease of provocation
will hardly guarantee an escape
to a cozy hell
rather, one should uproot the landscape
like a pickpocket with a lisp
whispering into the black rushing water
of underground rivers spilling out
into polite society
as the tongue of the world spins
upon its axis
the rabble are no more than
empty chairs and the human form
no better than a goldfish bowl
perched upon a crutch
if one is to live the myth then one must
read the tracks alone
into the snow blue with swart footprints
(like a negative to Pound's
haiku "…Metro")
where there is nothing left
but the hoisting of the atlatl and the ruddied

voice of dawn at the hunt's first run—
the song of the arrow released into its
bold lament where the stag falls
like a black oak and the dogs
prance 'round the breath-steam…

these pterodactyl wings of amethyst
and basalt stretch between your elongated
fingers and will pull you through the minutiae
of a thicket faster than light thinks of its hunger
where no one will follow not
even your shadow not even
the memory of your own
walk upon the water

Numbers

My shoes, which have
marched upon your ancestors
round the next corner in a kiss
where the pavement wrinkles into
the skin of innumerable blades of grass
veining roots beneath the azure feet
of mink

This tired moon that clasps a wooden blanket
to its flame unfolds the butterfly
of arboreal sex with eyes
of lips foliating in a desert
where an army of riderless bicycles
renders moot the suffocation
of a star

My arcane smile from a splintered glass
gives birth to the details of folded speech
woven by a woman made of palm fronds
in whose mouthful of snow
the silver of a cloud ignites
the quiver in the eyes of a
peacock's tail

A lavender fragrance
steals the center of a lime,
the last kiss, and my days

that are numbered

a small earth tremor takes notice
of the air in my darkened cup
while a delicate entrepreneur
backlogs orders for false teeth
provoking a bloody civil war
between fish that thirst
and those whose dust
replicates forever and without end

$$\bigcup_{n=1}^{m}(X_n \cap Y_n)$$

Beneath this latex forest this skeletal imago
I wait with my hooves that have wandered
for centuries in your charming and grassy
hotel corridor where the dead
walk upside down
and all the dancing flowers shimmer
like a mirror
upon this vastness
this prison wall

King Midas' Touch

My night rose, my black rain
my maple seeds hung in winter like dried
moths spider-wound and waiting
to be devoured by the tree of
the old torchbearer King Midas
whose flame resembles a medallion
worn by schoolgirls when the villagers
sing to a panther in heat roaming
the streets in search of its luck
These animals slither
into the surrounding hills of stars
much to the amazement
of no one

The catacombs are filled each year
with devils and clowns who fight
for their limited number of masks
they play musical chairs on all fours
blood bellowing a drinking song
from the bottom of the sea
about a child that is born with horns
and is beaten to death
by all the other children

But King Midas wears a large birdcage
& runs across his moat
fanning the flames while
the tail feather eyes of peacocks
are strewn upon a bone yard made of promises
like a young equestrian whose corset consists
of a delicate leather only a bookbinder may love

The string of a lightbulb is pulled
and the golden asp of the ancients
appears since in reality it is
not a snake but a ritual
performed by a forgotten race
that speak in symbols
like a piece of fruit
balancing on the top
of one's head

"My daughter" cries Midas,
"is a giant praying mantis!"
but it's not much different
than an armored truck swerving
top heavy
into an abandoned alley where
her gentlemanly face is fashioned from a hat
and her goatee waxed to a fine
stiletto point that stabs
the holes of the universe open
as hands become rubber gloves
testicles x-rayed
and one's hide is transformed
for the Rational Barter

Everything the world calls Itself
will be poured into its rightful place
that is to say the King's pocket
where the last living creature the cockroach
offers a sad reproach to the mute bundles
of the disinherited like Little Bo Peep

who twines her mustache and sucks
a very large stogy

Road maps to oblivion
are delicately sewn to the skin
a morphine gauze trembling with
virginal excitement
"Last rites! Last rites!" begins
the coachman with the button eyes
but no one hears
and contrary to previous warnings
or common disbelief
this story always ends
in a whisper

Seated Harlequin

my hands have fingers by the bunches
and looking over a railing I have no fear
of tossing myself head first
should the doorbell ring answer it
and if you are greeted by a triceratops
covered in coarse blue hair
like a wicker laundry basket then look
for a man's head strolling by
impossibly propelled on two
tiny feet
pick him up and roll him like a china plate
down a hole into Bedlam's basement
where a pygmy Buddha made of sugared dates
sits like a warning above a strange door
soft as a spider
smiling blood plump
the lion is loose in the corridor
beyond where the stone steps meet the ocean
and a woman wearing only seaweed
with starfish for eyes reveals
and then parts her blue breasts
like a seagull oaring the air
a cannonball indefinitely suspended
in the apex of curvilinear time
a little girl pupating butterflies
and my hands like sheaves of wheat are bound
down at the police station
where they are incarcerated for impersonating
the hands of a pope

Darling, I'm Yours

Because she thought that everything
would be taken care of,
the spade has cut the little parasite
in two quite accidentally
and without malice
leaving its signature in the spine
of a bird in flight

because she thought that when all else fails,
she could still drag out a rosary
and fill her empty skull
with words of porcelain
instead of an azure sky with an amber
sun spinning inward forgetful
of the anise lamps that burn
in the apostasy of night

because the cuteness of her indolence
was quite acute,
shit stained bloomers became the rage
coiffed in an elegance by a chandelier
that blew sleet on the steel teeth
of insects in winter's grimace

because she thought that her table was set
the legs of a chair were ready to walk
into the wash-and-wear light of day
coruscating from a can of calves brains
in a bashful supermarket
where the skeletons blush from the
nakedness of a lost pair of gloves

because she thought that the way to win a ham
was to strike an incendiary pose
on the head of a match,
a fetus was ordained to be Republican
with certain unalienable rights
such as the right to bare money
assuming the sanctity of boyhood
and the will to pull
                   one's own
                          switch.

Straight Talk

Even in the non-light from your
painted cardboard fires, a residue of leer
betrays a poisoned face.

Frankly, I would not care to think
of a God whose grunting
manufacture produced a mud ball,
bathed in an ocean of tears because
he was lonesome.
We've paid for our life
with our life.
So why curse awareness? Isn't it
enough to have a ringside seat in
the body's quiet darkness that
surpasseth all understanding?

And if you had it to do over again wouldn't
you take another bite; wouldn't you pull all the
leaves from the Tree and replace them with
Words, just for a Laugh?

Death, after all, is never on time
but always on cue
making bad actors of us all
through the corniness of our dying.
Death is the bellhop in a seedy hotel
who hands you a message
on a tarnished silver plate standing
in your way while the object
of your desire slips naked
beyond your reach. So what
if the elevator doors close—
take the stairs.

All Kidding Aside

Death's mask
unmasks you

renders your codpiece
to an impotent rust

unties your bodice
releasing your ribs

takes the play that you've written
and unwrites it

The Betrothed

Have pity on the body
have pity on its darkness
on its hungers
have pity on this body
with its secrets
the big dumb animal
that loves you
that doesn't know any better
that tries to comfort you
keeping only itself
and you
happy
have pity on this body
that was sold a bill of goods
by something older
and wiser than itself
that was told to go out
into the world dressed only
in a garland of belief
left to wander in its
lust wounded
in its desire to want
more to have
more to touch
more to eat
more
to be
more
to want

Comedy

the young shoes
dance into the doorway
one shoe falls over
a large ball rolls away
the funny shoes
squeak into the doorway
one shoe falls over
the audience laughs on cue
the dark shoes
shuffle into the doorway
one shoe falls over
snake eyes on loaded dice
the angry shoes
crawl across the doorway
one shoe falls over
traces of blood in the hall
the strange shoes
swim to the doorway
one shoe falls over
blue shadows stretch
into infinity
the tragic shoes
stumble through a doorway
one shoe falls over
flames engulf the house
the golden shoes
escape from the doorway
one shoe falls over
flocks of birds released
into the radiance
entering Paradise

Entre chien et loup

Objects With Shadows

The sun cackling like a fish in broad daylight:
the moon overripe with the joints of bones

Young lightning encircles the globe:
a darkened bulb enticing the elderly

One feather stretched and multiplied in the cavern of ingots:
human lice devoured by the songs of lead cubes

Indolent clergymen coughing gray fedoras against a door:
the chiaroscuro of deep-sea fish with breasts translucent

Leaves unfurling into snakes in the Arctic breeze:
*at the center of the earth where man becomes woman, woman
    man*

The leaves with eyes, blameless in their judgment:
discarded halos ravishing the blind countryside

The cock's crow, cut upon the stone in disbelief:
a rose, ferocious in its appetite for red

A magnetic field sharpening its teeth:
wheat rusting the blood of a compass

The coquette of bones honored by a fireplace:
a seismograph for measuring wind chill

A fire of violets drowning in silence:
the blonde voice violent with water

Twin pools, darkened by hummingbird larvae:
the Cyclops renamed, conversing freely in mink

A voiceless otter asks wayward children for a map:
the unguarded gate, silent in its chatter

A vampire, holding an invisible object, walks upon the water:
two chairs and a table drift lifelessly to the bottom of the sea

My unknowable death mask, whose features resemble numbers:
the parking meter of my heart, milking the whiteness of a word

Why Space Is Pear-Shaped

The sonorous sea sneezes violins
and cellos ashore by the hundreds
from a myriad of typists submerged
in diving bells the world calls
oak.
The coral encircles it with a halo because
time is nonsense.
Now the lightning crabs that glide upon fingertips
denude the accordion winds of darkness
at midday—
now the statues sink knee-deep in sand
rusting like a pillar of stars
made of soft grass.
The water wears a cap when it's cold.
The squid ink of snow petal gills breathing red
wax lips of cut poppies that spring from
a floating chair whose legs
resemble the hands
of a clock.
Moths issue freely from the mouth.
You are the ventriloquist calculating
centigrade for the flower on the fruit
of the tongue for the heart
in the shape of an emerald.
The albino bat of evening's fetid milk
hangs right-side up in the gallery of blind umbrellas—
and the shirt un-ruffles the night in its folds;
a voice, curving mercurial pear-shaped space
by the eyeful.

Fata Morgana

I know of this abandoned water tower
    whose legs were known to strut on tiny feet,
where the rain collects like feathers in
    a damaged teacup,
sprouting the flowers
        that inhabit the mouth.

Inside, the children hold their breath underwater
    becoming birds,
measuring their years in isolated moments
and increments of bone.

That adolescent girl over there
 is a swallowtail mingled with the grace
of a young piano,
as the street lamp lit at noon becomes
      an idol for the sun
      the key of a star
left lonely by the angle of its lean,
inside an empty crystal.

The Blue Danube fills the water tower
 with an evening of azure birds,
      their memory of names breeding
      a matrix of locations.
A Trojan Horse coughs like a piranha
      when the emptiness of the hands
      are cupped
      shaping the heart of a cheetah.

Inside this heart lies a house

in the geometry of a room
where you sit
entangled in a language
       no one speaks.
The triangle is a flame.
The square is a gate.
The circle – a map for adventure.

The human form no longer exists
here and the bite of an amorous
viper rekindles a lost love,
       provoked by the shrill of the Kingfisher,
       distilled from the kisses his wife bestows,
         forever
       and in a state of departure.

Webster's*

Descriptions of a poem that
Set out to wear the
Jodhpurs of the world in a
Steady state of amnesia is like a
Gyroscope making love to a
Locofoco hot-head that needs a drink made from
Amanita inside the
Kiva where an Indian sits
Shapeless as a shadow that
Reintegrates the automobile's
Hypospadias direction – a
Proximate to the lethal
Malevolence that usually accompanies the
Lechery of the
Lurdane, which is not to say a
Berry is the legitimate heir of local
Flora since the problem is quite
Knotty and not without a certain
Metathesis.

*The first word of every line is selected chronologically by
chance from a dictionary.

Three Sidewalk Poems Rejected
by the City of Saint Paul

I

The dead walk beneath
our feet touching us in
mirror fashion or so
some poet has said but
I'd rather think of the Earth
as simply an obstruction
to that vast and unfathomable
black depth of stars
carpeting the soles of our feet.

II

It's a hot one. The
Earth turns its cheek
towards the hub of the sun
while shadows slice the street
into parcels of night. My
feet are frying. I'll stop
here in this shade, remove
one shoe and plunge my
foot into that oasis of a
snowbank that once was or
is yet to be.

III

Look at these ants.
And where are they marching to?
Each with their own
predestined stairway,
a step away from the hubris
into an apartment made
of their own blind searching.
And where does it end?
Somewhere at the end of a street
around a corner curved in a question,
past the lilac gates of evening,
through the doorway to a dream.

Sleepless Haiku

restless thoughts from nowhere
dreams   glimpsed, not entered
shadows of leaves on snow

Feathered Haiku

handsome   vultures   with
pink flamingo necks graceful
as   the   letter   "J"

Thunder

thunder is heard but ignored
while the rain gives applause
to the moment
and without meaning to give
any grandiose scheme
or malice of explanation
for the majestic quality
in the suchness of things
a person, not even a poet,
sits for centuries silhouetted
in the doorway
thinking about trees
forgetting what they are

Spider

to have had such a fierce
and solitary appetite that one
should devour the entire table
cloth and then rend it strand by
strand from one's heart pulling
out little pieces of forks,
cups, spoons, napkins
and a vase of long dead flowers
once admired by her mummified guests
all mixed with a strange and distant
sorrow that gets knitted back
into an inviting spread by
long ebony fingers of
fishing poles that
click, click, click
in a rhythmic
suture of the night
is to see oneself as
COMPLETE
both cause & effect
both master and servant
hunger being such an all
encompassing event that
it would overflow and
blend into love tucking
in her new guests her
victims injected with
a rare wine of Lethe
drowsing with an
inner fire
happily

The road of excess leads to the palace of wisdom

A dead body revenges not injuries

The weak in courage is strong in cunning

The tygers of wrath are wiser than the horses of instruction

Eternity is in love with the productions of time

Shame is Pride's cloke

Joys impregnate, sorrows bring forth

The bird a nest, the spider a web, man friendship

Winter Solstice

the few trembling leaves
of a darkened garden fall
anonymously into an ochre heap
the freeze that shapes my breath
descends upon the burdock
as the sun descends
a pearl
waiting for the diver in the black
of this year's end
the groundwater a magnet for the frost
coils the sensate traveler drawing
deep into the nautilus like speech
from your lover
in sleep
while somewhere a serpent made of light
ascends the ruddy Aztec stair
a tenuous geometry of
proof for a beckoning altar
with promises to keep

      but here the shadows stretch for miles
beneath a feeble welder's arc
whose rays the viper's tongue adores
      diminishing day
        and
      empowering night

The Snowflake Architecture of the Eye

The snowflake architecture of the eye
opens the concealed adornment
dripping from the vestibule of light
    arresting insects who enter
        as a widow
           black as frost

Before me, the milking of a great bonfire sets
the stars into foam by the invisible vertebrae of numbers
defying the bark of the dogwood
    that regulates the climate
        inside my skull
          at half-past one

O nights of ardor and perfume!
my heretic's paramour – a sublime disease of explosive
          laughter, coughing
    tiny white umbrellas numberless
        as the tentacles
      of an extinct and forbidden ocean

The fish that fly around my mouth
and in my mouth, the voiceless descent of young lightning
      insolent to the face of a clock
         baring its fangs
One could say then, that, "at such and such a time"
when the forest becomes visible only to the eye
      within the eye

when that which was commonplace appears fortunately as
        an enormous dung beetle rolling the world away
when a priori judgment on the solidity of a chair
        becomes the lion with its teeth in a cup
when everything becomes, only as I advance towards it
        and because I advance
when I have forgotten the sound of my own footsteps
        and the reassurance of that sound
then,
        Then…O my violent spider!

Desire
for Cass

with her hands of brittle turquoise
with her Egyptian hands
dipping
into the star-strewn ink of the Nile
swan arms that rise and fall
rise and fall blindly
into each backstroke unknown
even to themselves

with her ears of nautilus shell
in whose labyrinth the lightening
loves the sea
where rows of empty houses stand
desolate inviting
with rooms made of scattered winds
words flow into an abyss
of unlocked doors

with her nose of mauve
of gamboge and alabaster
a cape unfolds revealing the world

with her siren mouth of ice flowers
her tongue of a young bird
tongue of a pine tree carelessly watching the steam
from an approaching train
lips that I kiss of magnetic carbon
the voice of a caravan crossing the Alps

with her eyes of whispers
naked as young saplings in evening dress
where ospreys snag fish in a taxi
with her eyes vaccinating a tango
like the wig of a harpsichord her
eyes' iris an eclipse of the sun
in this marriage of totem
and abstraction
dancing on the
head of a
pin

Frank O'Hara

Frank caught his last taxi
at Dune and Ocean but
now it is beautiful again
outside
and pears can be eaten
down to their black
seeds
like a young bride.
The fountains are thrusting
buttermilk
into the blue
mouth of the sky again
but
what this world needs
is a good $2 pair of shoes
(how else to say it?)
Frank would have approved
since words were not
unfaithful
to him and
life
for what it's worth
could always
replace
them

Pinter Place

Harold I had wanted
or should I have?
to like your poems
unfancied in their clear light
like the Fairfield Porters your plays
reality not reality
and wondered what you may have thought
of mine or
should I have?
too darkled with ornamentation
you may have said but
I too have a straight razor
that slices nicely
no matter
the more I see of you now
that you are gone
the less I know
and like a popular soft drink
imaged on a desolate billboard
somewhere in Kansas you
are everywhere
invisible

William S. Burroughs
1914–1997

In the darkened secret room tower
of flesh flowers radioactive
cobalt blue air dissolving
the hydrogen keys of the sun
take two and call me in the morning
chameleon of the radiant shadows
whose sex of locusts sing
in a petrified forest the fossilized
pungency of star fragrance
don't look now boyz but these parasite
words survive with their nests intact
now you'll see 'em and now you don't
The ivory skeleton-chair hovering
translucent and wet as fresh
insect wings trembling
with the penumbra of the body's
final moment how often,
O white-knuckled heat of St. Louis,
have we met?
Calculating the cc's needed for a chlorophyll
fix of mistaken identity
needed for the summer's greening
& decaying in the paragraph of all this
so-called modern-talk
Hey!
look who's
pushing
up Daisy

Where Have you Gone?
for Benjamin Péret

Where have you gone with the pine tree's teeth slender
as a stalk of ice cream
breathing in a valley of blood oranges
when the filings of an iron coat adhere to the migration
of the flounder's eye, heavenly as a lady
dropping her dainty hanky
on a pole

Where have you gone with the justice of just lice
from the bone fires bigger than a box
of chocolate
the race horse of fortune's blight is cloaked
in careful trees of frostbite from a monkey's hand
while conjugal ellipses drown the forgotten tooth
of the hair-brained trigger figure
my brain skates an oval empire
in front of a forest pallid as the day is long
The coaxial formulae for flowers twists
on the buttocks of sheep who vote
for all the money they are worth, saying:
    eat me, your sins have been absolved
    drink me, I'm perspiring like a pig.

But where have you gone, endemically speaking
of course, like a ladder to a shoe horn
a worm to a hitching-post
when the green tips of gangrene eyes point
jealously to the fishbone caught

in the throat I mean the needle
of a compass worn thin as a haystack,
thin as a necktie
worn by a blizzard.

The fruit of your fall is the shadow
of a ringless hand the echo of bearded
moonlight crawling in an attic.
There, where the evening coat is empty,
shouldered by a wooden hanger whose
personality is divine whose mica
dust resembles the pattern of a
Saturday Night Special
or the writing on the leaves of water lilies
          gliding past the tomb—
          beneath the saturation of stars
          that burst into flame ψ

Twilight Dirge and Exeunt

Even the night's fetid glance
cannot dispel the blindness in a species
without hope.
Eyes that foliate and darkle
a flowering lava beneath my feet,
gliding upon a road of naked tendrils
where I am far
and away
inhabiting
my own silhouette.

The Liquid Night

Cyclops

The moon is an oyster on the half shell
weathered edges knife
the lanterned curtain of night
slicing an invisible arc…
brutal fuel for a heatless lamp thou
art an abstracted eye that
picks apart
the human heart.

☪

Tonight the heavens are in crystal
as clouds issue from my breath
and I walk the earth with hell
in my head—
sparks flying in my wake
through a density of
ice black air
consumed with self
in my own
myopian ooze
I stop
and smooth
my hair.

Night Trees for Hugo (Dislocations)

Hugo Ball's trees were called what they seemed,
heavy laden with rain and sleep
they became even more,
"pluplusch
        and
pluplubasch,"

but why call them anything why
not say that they have simply arrived
well dressed and ready
for a final curtain call

What will the new word be what
will the new snow cover like a sunrise;
the Opiliones swagger on stilts a mile long
under leaf
while we graze above on the warm light,
drunk in the wreckage of
our consciousness.
A language has washed up at my feet—
a debris of objects sans shadows;
let them speak freely rolling pebbles
with their tongues
bewitched by birds darting
forever and invisibly with their fish
scales sloughed of meaning
mirrors of feldspar orbiting
the faces that stare
under a firmament rich in possibilities
of no end.

I no longer feel this location

I only feel this earth.
Saturated, I sleep in my mother's arms,
my bed full of moonlight and indigo
                    while outside
Hugo's last tree sits silhouetted
by a much vaster darkness
issuing from the raking
notes of a cricket
          with his black
                    oilskin rainbow
                              music box.

The Ocean

…spits its teeth on the beach lapping
foam from an old dog's tongue
the young bird's eye hovering
devouring children in a drowning song

…as orange as the moon is distant
sweeps night into a prandial indigo
for the mouth of blood-tide hissing
exhaling a perfume of stars

…with its beautiful and invisible hand
rising like an emerald fire
where the guillotined head rolls
into the musk of the dark basket

…is an insect that comes and goes
comes and goes watching the silk
white dress tumble in slow motion
disembodied through the viscosity
of its silent sinking

…betrays a softness in its voice
inside the steel trap of beckoning
pink lady slipper starfish mouth
abstracting flesh into space becoming

…rolls rocks round and seashells spit
feeds the shore with a broken punctuation
of lost love and love yet
to be fathomed.

The Ocean II (reprise)

spits its teeth on the lapping beach
foam froth from an old dog's tongue
the moon orange as the night becomes
exhaling a perfume of stars

foam froth from an old dog's tongue
a guillotined head for the dark musk basket
exhaling a perfume of stars
in an ancient drowning song

a guillotined head for the dark musk basket
with its beautiful and invisible hands
in an ancient drowning song
a fire of emeralds cresting

with its beautiful and invisible hands
the white silk dress sinks to oblivion
a fire of emeralds cresting
like an insect that hisses your name

the white silk dress sinks to oblivion

feeds the shore with its broken communion

like an insect that hisses your name

for the indigo blood tide kissing

feeds the shore with its broken communion

like a lover extinguishing sorrow

for the indigo blood tide kissing

rolls rocks round to their diamond core

spits its teeth on the lapping beach

with its beautiful and invisible hands

a fire of emeralds cresting

the moon orange as the night becomes

Silence

A house thickens with the darkness and becomes leaden by the sudden departure of one's spouse into a profound sleep. The quickening silence secures the space, accentuated by the few remaining sounds that swim disconnectedly. A moth beats like a hummingbird heart against the interior of a lampshade as it orbits the nuclear bulb; a neighbor's dog yelps because the wind, facile and *utterly impersonal*, has shifted like a swinging door. Trees are no longer green grounded masts of roiling foliage but have become massive and move in closer with the predatory darkness. They loom in towards the tiny house as if they were the walls of a giant room. Inside the room, the house now sits tucked far and away in a blind forgotten corner. Transformed by the dim light of stars, the walls become translucent, waver, and mix into the fragments of night.

Evening Star

in the evening
in warmest lampshade hour
when the books are insects that fly from the shelves
like the bitter wind of the Silk Road vanishing
into the dust of Mongolian darkness
where the Sirens are mute in my
submerged library of drowned colors
where the stars create the first letter
of the word used to describe my life
this lexicon of assurances is short one
chair at the elemental table whose legs
skeletal from the first blue love of day
stand as evidence for the arsonist
in love with an earthly radiance
the sensual rills of ganglia in a whale's brain
are as much proof of the banister's descent
as the veins of an umbrella swelling
with the pregnant wind
which is spotted
and like a tarantula moves
across my bed in a very familiar way
almost comically
as if to say the fruit of a purloined
freedom is to desire the hermetic
of a sealed room
inside a secret house
where the weather resides in a cupboard
and the wallpaper licks you
as you pass by

The Vampire's Gift

If there is any pleasure in the consuming darkness

then it is through the propane flame

      of the vampire's gift

transmitted

   through the down turned hand & placed

       (sans sanguinarily)

    over the heart ♠

  solemn

    as a nipple in a teacup,

 and secret   as a mouthful of keys.

The deadly routine of the iridescent tulip's

    nascent grip

    prolongs the frost,

   lovely in its way to a mistress.

The penumbral darkness around her lips

    in the aureole of evening

  when the Sphinx rises from its haunches Ω

    offering her teats.

The vampire's gift is a bicycle saturated

    with the eagle's talons;

  an algorithm of trees singing to a blind man

      in a lamp-lit and decapitated

          stagecoach.

  It is the longing for a great distance,

    inside the diamond cloud that loves

       the enormity of a flea

         enchanted

     by a quiver of tiny white bones

   made of tinsel.

  It is the necromancy of an initialed

       handkerchief   Ψ

  where the night is a flesh puddle

draped as a shadow on your arm

   in the acrid light

     of midday's dust

       and naked,

   as the waters of the tongue.

Advice to an Insomniac

You must first capture the wreckage
with your legs,
arms akimbo frame
the impenetrable image—
forget the music of the day.
Remember the fierceness
     of your presence
         as an infant
            (and feed upon it)

When your head becomes a stack of wheat
and the feet
are stone round as two
ostrich eggs
(who let the silver reindeer onto the subway?)
say goodbye—
and fling yourself over
that unfathomable edge
of your bed.

Sleep is a junco
hopping in the snow
do not move
     and it
         will eat
            from your hand.

Sans Titre III

The (the)

(white) not white (not) black,
assuredly,

grey (curvilinear) orange

aspect;

      of the tippler's giddy roam
      of the line that takes itself for a walk Paul Klee

      of the flock revealed in the ancient tongue

            & the secret of birds

      of the flight (that is) not flight (today)
            the eleventh of July

          whence cicadas

rich   in   their
            sweetvelvet   bloom

      having waited (for) their (moment)

revel in the ancient tongue   in a ratchet of heat

(this)
a bouquet of sea-lions

85

and the last train the last watchman the last keeper of the
last gate where the last street lamp of the last hour in the
last night beneath the last star as the last man and the last
woman take their last stroll around the last corner of the
last building in the last town before the last forest of their
last mystery in the last of these Night Palaces
unbound, unbridled & unkempt

your eyes in combustion (forget)

walking unchained to the banquet

(celestial)

light from the dark vulva

and
one
finger
touches
(the water)
((rippled circle))
(((the orb within the orb)))
((((as time hesitates unmoved))))
(((((tenuous, ameliorated & breathless)))))

THIS
(not that
it was
meant
for what
it was
thought
not
to have
brought) &

                    THAT
                  (which,
                  was not
                   meant
                  for what
                   it was
                  thought
                  to have
                    had
                  as an
                 outcome)

stretches in abundance the landscape unfettered
an unconcealed quickening
of the body and of its vertical flight engendered
by a gaze that reaches out to the horizon pulling
the curvature of the earth towards you and
the undisputed truth that you are falling skyward
through the blue and roiling wind
like a runaway kite –
such is the life of the poet lived
in a dream to be standing naked
in a crowd
and yet have very few who
will
            ever
                   take
                      notice
beauty not made from language
but from the color of water which has
no color save of a molten reflection
of flint against steel, the piercing of sound
into vision,   the   fire   from   whence
            cometh
                       no
                                 words

ψ seeing figures or scenes ⇑ in the debris of the streets and realizing ⊙ they come from last night's dreams π for example a smashed cigar Д more than resembles a large stick insect Ж from a dream ф it really is the insect metamorphosed Џ in the light of day to resemble a smashed cigar Θ wherein one would see it come alive Ω given the subtraction of the rational mind Δ

meanwhile, summer grafts its skin to your eyes
                    and the bell is the breast of the door

dawn's drunken shore is smote
                    with ashes (and) calculations that
                                        the shadow bound clock
unveils like a white
            enflamed mask of the gods
                        (the face) that I enter each morning

            (there are only so many masks to go around
            I once saw a man walking about with no
            mask it was dreadful and unmerciful a
            horrible rawness of head with no face one
            had to ask why the unkindness what
            libation to what god had been missed? what
            signs had his subconscious misread;
            fomenting
                        into a complete
                                    loss of faith)

```
a       s       u       o       i       a
n       t       p       f       n       l
d       i       o               n       i
    l       n       g       o       k
y       l               u       c       e
e               t       i       e
t       r       h       l       n
    a       e       t       t
l       i           y
i       n       f
g       s       a       a
h           c       n
t           e       d
            s
```

in the wind's unfurled tongue

        o child of nothing

                down at water's edge

where pubescent girls

        hurl rocks

            (at)tacking seagulls

and where the forfeiture

        of substance

            is not belief

        but instinct

and the barbarians are hoisting wing
leathered in their seaman's caps
faces bright, enameled gold
with azure fired eyes of Paradise
they glimpse the key to the sun
magnetic winds that carve
a mocárabe of light
into the milk of night…

                              …dappled among
                              the white branches
                              the icy butter of dawn

Icarus never fell
Jatayu saved his life
so take your own
walk upon the water…
lest your angels freeze
from fear

Two Essays

Ruralurban

Where am I? Half in jest, and with all due respect to *Nadja*'s opening lines, "Who am I," for it is clearly in the shadows of that remarkable and obscure light that I would wish to share the joke, the question is not without serious consequence in the answer. It would seem that Breton's use of the proverb, "Tell me whom you haunt and I'll tell you who you are," could be inverted, telescoped through surrealism's looking glass for the purpose of revealing the chimeras of one's interior as they graze upon the countryside. Tell me *where* you are, and I'll show you *how* it's haunted.

I was first attracted to the idea of "landscape" not from any sense of beauty, nor of its singularity, but rather for its unique ability to disappear and be taken for granted. The rural plebeian may disagree with me, saying that he would not live anywhere else, that he "loves" nature, and that he finds beauty in the ruggedness of his abode or in the animals he likes to plug. Yet, the creek behind his house is filled with abandoned refrigerators, rusted oil barrels and a rotting automobile. The farmer will find beauty in nature tamed, in a landscape of predictability and not, assuredly, in profitless possibilities. The silhouette of a particular mountain, the chance survival of a certain tree, or the rarity of a flower are facts that may be acknowledged by the ruralite and yet equally anesthetized—for nature, scrupulous in its illusion of Eternity, has rendered concrete in Westernized man an insensibility. The exigencies of nature are bathed in its own camouflage and a mind, filled with hallucination, will cease to hallucinate upon walking into the specularity of a woods. In other words, we think we own the place.

Conversely, I have been witness to quite a few peculiar sensations of a spectral nature while living in a city. For example, the sight of a corrugated hose laying in the street once presented itself not as something that *looked* like the rotting organ of some animal but rather that it *was* the rotting part of something—yes, perhaps an animal—and that, had I been in a forest, that same form would have presented itself in the same way and at the same time and place. Or, again, the form of a smashed cigar flattened into bits on the sidewalk so much resembled an insect from a dream that I was convinced it really was that insect come to visit the waking world. I repeat, tell me where you are and I'll show you how it's haunted.

Let's take New York City for instance, or, for the sake of clarification and in honor of its native bird, the Rock Dove (the pigeons were there before anyone, nesting in the cliffs), we'll call it Rock Dove Cliffs (RDC). RDC is in a very rural setting. I say this because, despite what appears to be waves of crowds, there are very few people there. Doomed as they are with this inward magnetization, where nothing matters outside of a fifty mile radius, or west of the Hudson as they say, the masses are forever living in a movie of their own design wherein everyone's a star and yet no one has anything more than a bit role. A multitude of locks are in place up and down the doors and, really, after being exhausted by a deluge of people, who wants to go out and see any more of them? This paradox washes out like a wind and generates a homogenous feeling of being

94

absolutely alone. One becomes unreal—a shade. Small wonder then that Breton felt quite alone, exiled as he was in Green Witch.

The brutal frankness of this wilderness is echoed in its skyline that resembles not so much the obvious set of broken teeth as it does the *sensation* of falling through an elevator shaft. Giant insects, of various metallic lustres, careen between the digital canyons both night and day. You can use them for transportation by climbing inside, just behind their wing-plates. Their eyes glow in the dark. When the rain comes, weaving gray and greasy sheets through the canyons, large bats may be seen emerging from their caves in the cliffs. Their wings are for shelter, not flying. They scamper between the cliffs in a fashion of mushrooms; some are brightly colored but mostly they are black. The earthy smell of the rain lends weight to the illusion of their existence; the clinging wetness of clothing transforms the figures into aerodynamic shapes of rabbit bone. Underground, a wild and immense worm thunders through its tunnels. You can feel the earth shake when it goes by. If you are standing near its vent on the surface, you may feel the feculent expiration of the beast wash over you in a warm brown air. Perhaps the generic smell of the entire island comes from these holes—it's neither pleasant nor foul, but rather a cancellation of odors that leaves a peculiar residue; the perfume of hot electrical wire mixed with a faint hint of glucose.

Not everyone is unreal—there are some survivors such as artists, poets, etc. However, this is not to say that all artists are real. Jewelry Snobble, for instance, who had been in the spotlight in the early eighties and went on to produce a (what else?) movie about a now deceased artist named

Basquiatwarhol, had truly been the darling of all the self-licking culture ghosts lined up for their ration of Art-Pablum. Just as the French loved to dig up Rimbaud, so too shall we take to our shovels. Nothing revolutionary about Basquiatwarhol though, is there? Despite a supposed "refreshing" naïveté, the work is rife with blatant clichés. It's an emotive display rendered moot through repetitive gestures that display a tragic ennui via feigned artistic process. The world called him a genius and he believed it so he kept doing the same thing over and over. Am I saying the work is bad? No, simply immature and accompanied by the attendant romanticizing of a squandered life which, by the way, is rather textbook. Here's another tragic figure of a young artist done in by the Art Hype. These New Clothes for the Emperor are meat for the hungry ghosts, and the royal wardrobe may be viewed in the scullery of every Whitney Biennial.

The postmodern art world is nothing more than a Victorian beach, awash with the electric eels and rays of a bygone avant-garde. Heavily dressed bathers re-clad in their striped suits are poking through the debris with their toes. The so called simplest surrealist act of firing a gun into a crowd has become, unfortunately, quite literal and commonplace. And likewise for the art world, nothing shocks. We've come to expect anything and be entertained by it, rather than healed, for the shamans are dead. The art world is ruled by academicians now (if you want to be $uccessful at it, go to Yale). Pick up any Sunday newspaper and peruse the "Arts & Entertainment" or "Arts & Leisure" sections wherein one may still find the rational positivism of the late 19th century. Let us sing the corporate anthem then, of all the young eager beavers in Mass Media who help us develop our thoughts. Let's use Aragon's accordion for accompaniment. Do you remember the tune? Of course you don't. The melody is written prettily on the bellows. Shh…I can almost hear him playing it:

MASS MEDIA

We squeeze the instrument and make some letters disappear:

MSS MEDA

and then open it again

MASS MEDIA

MSS MEDA – MASS MDIA – MSS MEDIA

MASS MEDA – MSS MDIA – MASS MEDI

ASS MEDIA

ASS MED

SM

Oh my, the bellows
are a bit cracked… $ ME

A$$ ME

A$$$$ MED

MA$$$$$$$...$$$$...MEEEEEDIA…

And so on.

But perhaps the savagery, that is to say the poetic spirit that has kept art alive, is only sleeping. There are beautiful paintings to be found all over the island of Rock Dove Cliffs that the hungry ghosts are incapable of seeing. Da Vinci's instruction for his pupils to take a paint-soaked sponge and hurl it at a wall for the purpose of making a landscape manifests itself in the unthinking gestures of an MTA worker who has given the hundredth coat of non-color paint to a small patch above an anonymous door. And there, at a subway station around Times Square, up in the corner attended by a bare lightbulb, is a picture of Hannibal crossing the Alps. One of his elephants has died and now he must take its skull and drain the whiteness from it if the blizzard is to stop. Or, over there, next to the dumpster that's been recently used to clear a space for yet another speculative $ art $ gallery ("We were going to open either a restaurant or an art gallery and art galleries are easier cuz they're just an open space") is a picture of Little Red Riding Hood arranging the bones of her grandmother in a picnic basket for the Wolf. Or, here, where fossils sprout wings and radiate around an entwined pair, with a toothy smile, and a handful of glass crickets. And when I say these things, it is not that they look *like* this or that, it is always that they *are* that, because poetic experience that is lived does not rely on metaphor to make its presence known—it supersedes it, as liquid reality supersedes logic. Likewise, the Poet is not necessarily one who writes since living a poetic life is sufficient.

The transformative nature of words, regardless of the language or the design of their skeletal letters (or, for that matter, the way in which the lymph vowels are placed, the syntax-spleen harbored, etc.) may, however, be our only

98

signpost for the exit. As Eluard had noted, *words do not lie.* Each letter has an origin whose existence has little to do with its present day appearance and thus each word carries a latent meaning capable of evolving the language. It is a concrete entity that extracts its name from your lips. We do not name things; we sound them out as best we can for they are already named. They are a palimpsest that evokes the creation of myths.

But, I am drifting. I wanted to talk about the landscape, how the rural and urban environments are intermingled, how the mysteries of night reside in the shadows of day, how abstract Nature truly is…but right now I am having a memory of one of the most densely populated areas on the planet. I am thinking of Arches National Monument in Utah and the surrounding area. Anyone who has ever been to these parts will agree that the immensity of Nature, which chooses to display here in the rawest and most refined of manners, creates an overwhelming sense of impermanence for the hairless apes that go scurrying about from damp hole to shady grove— spouting their tiny worldviews and truncated narratives with utmost importance. It is here, in the seeming endlessness of the landscape, that one feels crowded by the convergence of various world cultures found etched and sculpted into rock. Of course, the tourists have taken thousands of photos of every sculpted rock that resembles something in their deranged lives—oh, that one looks like my dog, that one looks like my cousin Ernie, ad nauseam. You may even be unfortunate enough to take the Colorado River night boat tour offered there. It advertises a "light show" for the feeble minded in case they don't understand how the game is played. But, be warned: the silent laughter you think you may be hearing inside your skull as you drift through the darkness (with all the other squeaky clean and deodorized mostly white folk out for a good time) is not imaginary. The rocks are howling at your stupidity so laugh with them, lest one decided to fall on you or worse—that you become blind to the totality they represent. Metaphor, in the hands of the infantile, raises its hind end in the form of the word *like*. I'm sorry, these rocks are not up for interpretation. The fissures and striations that run through the entrada are an unknown alphabet passing before your eyes at such a high speed that they seem frozen into the rock. They are the graphic representation of every myth known and combine to form new myths yet to be created. And some of them are quite alien. All of this resides at the base of the brain—if only you had the key. I have little doubt that Artaud, despite his paranoia (or because of its blessing) made a correct assessment of the Tarahumara when he said that, "If the greater part of the Tarahumara race is indigenous, and if, as they claim, they fell out of the sky into the Sierra, one may say they fell into a *Nature that was already prepared*. And this Nature chose to think like a man. Just as she *evolved* men, she also *evolved* rocks," and also, "there are places on the earth where Nature, moved by a kind of intelligent whim, has sculpted human forms."[1]

Driving into the Arches, one feels as though one were entering a vast metropolis. A fanfare reminiscent of Rachmaninoff's "Isle of the Dead" seems to sound from the blood-red pillars of rock that loft themselves into the carapace of blue sky and white cloud. Sculpted forms

---

[1] Antonin Artaud, *Selected Writings*, ed. Susan Sontag (New York: Farrar, Straus and Giroux, 1976; reprint, Berkeley: University of California Press, 1988).

combine into skyscrapers with the dual function of monument. Here the goddess Isis comforts her double Hathor. Thoth and Amon debate with Krishna the heretic Prometheus. Kokopelli converses freely with Urizen. A Balanced Rock commemorates Magritte; distant mesas celebrate Max Ernst and the idea of his *Petrified City*. Is it not ironic that, in the middle of nowhere, one may feel in touch with a myriad of cultures; a crowded Grand Central Station of the Titans. Taking a jeep out of Moab and into the foreboding Martian terrane will yield a further telling of the great myths and all their sordid subplots. Nature's monument to Entropy, which masquerades as Time, is observed here in the strictest silence. The ruins are immense, the narcotic of oblivion quite personable.

These vast networks of petrified energy were *read* by the ancients and culminate in nodes of pictographs. The nodes are distributed by chance—some are quite beautiful, all of them quite mysterious. They are visions painted with gypsum and other minerals, mixed with the fat of the kill. They are also computer monitors, connected to the gods whose blood colors the rock, whose white and azure hair color the sky. Likewise the dreams of these people (as the dreams of all people) may be compared to a computer program, downloaded by nature. Every night we are faced with learning a new computer skill. The structure is the same, only the software and information changes. Access to the source, and gaining a more insightful level, is supplied through lucid mode, which is not an easy task for most dreamers who forget their file menu options and end up just watching the screen saver. Is it not ironic though, that the figuration of dreaming should, in the most Hegelian of terms, manifest itself in broad daylight through the guise of a computer model? That a culture whose fear and denial of the power of dreaming should find its apparition staring them in the face of every day of every work week? Of course, what am I talking about? most people deny that they even have dreams.

However one may feel about dreams, the physiognomy of the landscape is something that cannot be ignored. The American Southwest is only one extreme case—the cypresses of Italy, for example, display similar attributes of the desert rock in their role as sentinel or guardian, i.e., their similarity rests in the fact that *they are watching us*. And if we are being watched, it is because we do not watch ourselves. Nature has the ability to disappear and be taken for granted. And, in much the same way, the ignorance of ourselves creates an erasure whose only restoration will be realized through the dialectic and conciliation of opposites. The familiar refrain in the folk song that *this land was made for you and me* is an unmerited assumption. I must tell you that this land is mine—and that I refuse to share it. Unless, of course, you care to internalize it—in which case, it is yours.

The Inflated Tear

Many artists listen to music when they are in the solitude of the studio. Whatever you choose to listen to is reflective of that inner environment wherein one taps the creative wellspring. For some it's classical, for others it's rock, etc. Jazz, for me, has always been that catalyst and support needed to make those leaps of faith so necessary when one is involved particularly with abstract painting. I think it's the improvisational nature of jazz that makes it so available to my creative process. That loose and yet structured balance that is jazz is in complete agreement with my own studio aesthetic. I feel like I'm a musician who paints. And the idea that jazz is still concerned with making what we call "beauty" underlines my own poetic sensibilities. I think that's something that's actually been missing from the art world for some time now. In fact, one is taught in art school that beauty is suspect. That, to be concerned with it, is to accept all the cliché that attends it since beauty is something we must agree upon in order for it to be recognized as such (and, therefore, no surprises, no new direction). Musicians, on the other hand, actively seek it. Has listening to jazz made me a better artist? Possibly.

Rahsaan Roland Kirk, more so than anyone else, really speaks to me as a visual artist. And this is all the more ironic for his blindness. I know he didn't like being reminded of this and, so far as I can tell, he could "see" just fine. In fact he saw better with his ears than most do with their eyes. I have no trouble believing that he was creating shapes and narratives in his mind – a synergy of aural and optical elements to create one thing possessing both tragedy and humor. And the more lucid you are in this way, as a creative spirit, the greater your expanse of theatricality. Rahsaan was a painter of inner worlds let loose through his horns.

In his piece "The Inflated Tear" there is a very powerful flow of imagery going on that I don't think he, nor anyone else I know of, ever talked much about. The song (in the version from the album, *The Case of the 3 Sided Dream in Audio Color*) starts with a brief and innocent intro of a wiry melody reminiscent of the nursery song "London Bridge is Falling Down". This is abruptly interrupted by what one can only describe as a freight train coming out of nowhere. But, as the freight train disappears, this initial section is followed by a lush and gorgeous panoply of notes that, nevertheless, manages to transform itself into a percussive round of tension that returns us to the freight train and a reprise of the childish intro – this time on a toy piano playing the first few notes of "Strangers in the Night". The lush section repeats and flows into more tension along with Rahsaan calling out "Help him! Help him! I don't know what's happening, I'm sorry but…" At least that's what I think he says. Anyway, it all fades out after this and all the sounds become very small. Of course, Kirk was blinded at an early age by a nurse putting too much medicine in his eyes and I think this song is the reenactment of the event: the child's intro, the abrupt feeling of enormous surprise in the freight train, the false sense of well-being in the lush melody that transforms into tension, the injected humor of "Strangers in the Night" and the call for help by who? the nurse? his mother Gertrude?

All of this makes for a work of art that expresses both tragedy and an existential sense of humor. It's one of my favorites.

An abstract painter doesn't need to look at nature for encouragement as the creative spirit has its own life. An abstract painting should stand on its own and, like nature, have its own existence and be its own thing. When I started the painting titled "The Inflated Tear (for Rahsaan)", it didn't occur to me that I was going to dedicate it to the song or to the Kirk influence. I never start out knowing what's going to happen and I don't believe you should make a work of art that does little more than illustrate or interpret. Like I've said, it's a matter of improv – you lay down an element or a structure and you react to that like a jazz musician and keep going. I've noticed however that, try as one might, it is almost impossible to keep to a non-objective imperative and negate the image. Images surface as in a waking dream. Perhaps I was listening to Kirk's song when I was painting this, I don't remember. But at a certain point I noticed specific forms occurring: the mystical eye-hand in the center that plays on a horn, a cacophonic rhythm of shapes balancing on a fulcrum-neck, and the general African sculpture look and feel of the whole just seemed to point to Kirk. The lavender tear drop in the center (next to the eye-hand) was the only conscious piece added to the composition after I had decided on its title.

In an interview, Dorthaan Kirk said that her husband didn't adhere to any religion other than a "religion of dreams" (the name "Rahsaan" came from a dream). This type of spiritual self reliance is crucial for the creative individual and reminds us that to protect our own creativity requires a reliance on and a memory for those childhood instincts. Rahsaan very often injects his compositions with melodies and sounds both innocent and primal. I like it when he said that, "I didn't ask my mother to buy me a trumpet or a violin. I started right on the water hose."

I would say, for my own work, that jazz helps to keep the faith and the dream alive and that, at best, I should strive to paint like a child – only better.

Previously published as "A Note on the Cover Art" in *Brilliant Corners: A Journal of Jazz & Literature*, (Winter 2012): page 4.

A Note about the Author

Rollie Erickson is an artist who has exhibited work both nationally and abroad in such places as The Alternative Museum in New York and SPACES in Cleveland, Ohio. Juried exhibitions include diverse venues such as the Fayetteville Museum of Art, and the Barrett House Galleries—selections by Laura Rosentsock, then curator at the Museum of Modern Art (MOMA) in New York. Erickson's work has been reproduced in various catalogs and in *Art in America, 1984-85 Guide to Galleries, Museums, Artists*. He has received grants and honorariums from Artists Space, SPACES, and Dance Theater Workshop. In 1995, he founded and published *Wordimage*, a one-time literary magazine that explored the relationship between text and imagery as well as contemporary surrealist poetry. Featured visual poets included John Bennett, John Vieira, and Irving Weiss. A copy resides in MOMA's library collection. Rollie and his wife Cass, a playwright, currently live in St. Paul, Minnesota.

www.ingramcontent.com/pod-product-compliance
Lightning Source LLC
Chambersburg PA
CBHW072127090426
42739CB00012B/3100